FOOD FOR LIONS

Dedicated to

Shawn, Melissa & Tiffany

CONTENTS

NOTE TO THE READER

Here we are, together in this moment. Welcome. I hope the words you find on these pages speak to you in all the ways you need. May they soothe your hunger pains for a brighter world and allow you to brave whatever season of life you currently find yourself. I've organized the passages of this book in the order of *Unraveling, Inner Exploration, Mantra & Self*, and *Lovers*.

Unraveling speaks to the deconstruction of my life. Like many, I realized that my mental and emotional foundation needed mending. Ultimately, it ended up in a complete reconstruction. Like any rebuild, there is a demolition process. It felt like death, but now I can appreciate and hold gratitude for this time. If this is where you currently find yourself, I urge you to keep sifting and sorting through this painful time. I know how tempting it is to want to throw in the towel.

Inner Exploration is a window into my spiritual work. My practice is centered around seeking the highest possible wisdom I can grasp and being present. I gain insights from every encounter, but I glean most of my guidance from observing nature. With its seasonal transformations, cyclical patterns, and ability to hold space for all, nature has shown its wisdom to me repeatedly.

Mantra & Self is about focus. These words help center, ground, and expand my thinking. Coming from a background rife with trauma, I've found that building phrases for grounding and centering help break anxiety loops. Breaking these loops allowed me to become more present in my life. Being present prompted a deep desire to expand my understanding of self and how I relate to the world around me. So, you'll find questions I spent many months contemplating and journaling about. If one of these prompts sticks with you, I highly encourage you to take the time to write out your thoughts. There is so much to learn about you.

The entire book is built on the idea that everything is love, but in *Lovers,* you will find passages about the evolutions of love in light of romance. You know, all the sad sappy goodness. It's difficult not to wax poetic about this vibration of love.

My sincerest hope is that you have as many present moments as possible in this life and that these words aid you on your journey.

"UNRAVELING"

Our greatest lessons
in Love
Come from those
we didn't
Choose to love

The world keeps turning
I can't keep up
Faster and faster
It seemed
Till it stopped
For a moment
I was frozen
Feet fused to the floor
Where to next?
To impress
To excite
To move forward
To live life
Cuz we blink
And its gone
Now forever locked
In the past
Only able to visit
In my mind
I do it all the time
Over and over
It plays
Till my teeth grit
And I shake
Shake it off
I'm fine
Strut my stuff
Watch all fall
In line
I'll keep pushing
Till I find
My groove and
Feel I've got
Nothing to prove

Silence is a funny thing
Cuz once its here I want it to leave
Maybe because it's not distracting
From the voices that haunt me
So I'll pick up this pen
And I'll scratch down a few words
So the sound of pen to pad is all to be heard
Sleep deprivation plagues me
I know it's my brain just trying to save me
From the torture that awaits
Deep breath now you won't feel a thing
So I walk around all stressed out
And everyone keeps asking me how
I'm doing, fine I lie
Just to bide my time

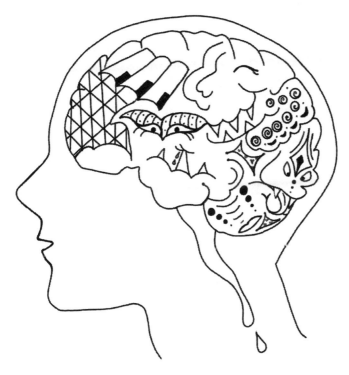

There was music playing

But I couldn't hear it

-DISSOCIATION-

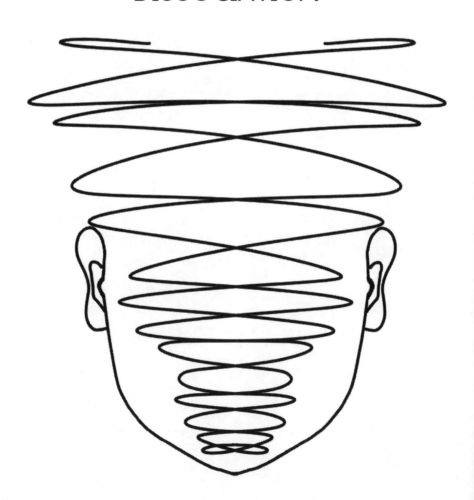

It's the age old tale
Silent anger in a pale
Faced child lost
In this world
Only now I want answers
Now I demand them
No more hiding
No more silence
No more sadness
Anger has morphed
Into rage and I've let
It out of its cage
To destroy all in my way
So step back or
You'll become its prey

It's done and I didn't even feel it
My blood it spills and flows
Too fast to heal it
The smell of iron the vibrant color
Splatters and smudges all over
But only a small moan do I utter
I've lost too much to catch up
But that's life suck it up
Get off the floor and put on a show
Dance little puppet that's all you know
Don't look at the blood it will only distract you
Without me you'd be nothing I built you
Now don't slip and hold onto this guilt
It's heavy yes but it's chained to your hip
So don't fight just slowly drift
As you go cold and your body goes stiff
Now I'll rock you to sleep such a good girl
Close your eyes you won't hurt anymore
Drift as your demons are set free
Covered in red its what's best you see

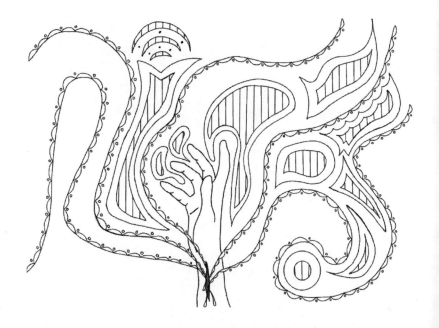

It's not fair
No, but not much is
You praise me but remind me I'm not perfect
You apologize yet ask me to aid you in your time of need
Even when what your struggling with causes me pain
I speak and you can only absorb a fraction of what I say
But is it right for me to be angered by this
How do I untangle myself from you
I need my head space back
I don't want to do this dance anymore
I want to say that your "sorry" didn't come too late
But I'm unsure

Even after I've cut off

All the parts of me

That fall outside the lines

I still don't fit

Why did I do this?

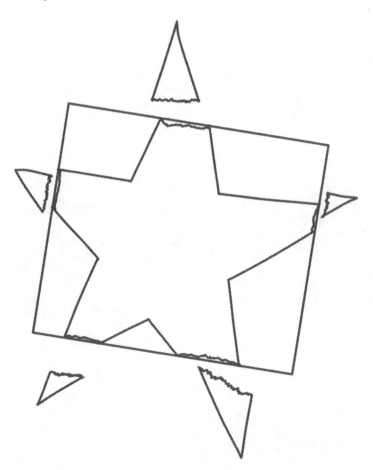

Don't look away
You need this

I'm vomiting truths
Nothings amiss

You hate it
You fight

I'm sorry
I won't lie

Turn your cheek
See what happens

I'll spit in your face
Pay attention

Cuz you did this
So selfish

Say you're sorry
Couldn't care less

Your motives
Are unclear

Can't open my heart
That's my greatest fear

I hate your smile
And your laugh

And what hurts most
Is that's all we had

I thought you would be the one I had to bury

But I see that's not the case

I'm left holding the shovel to bury

The part of me you created

The part of me that wanted to believe

Your lies so desperately

It's a bitter pill to swallow

Don't worry (not that you would)

I'll sing songs of praise for her

As she protected us from

Your ugly truths for so long

I'll dress her in the finest silk

And surround her with fragrant flowers

As she takes her last breaths

Through the pain of this death

I'll be right by her side till the end

When she has returned to the earth

I'll grieve not for her death

But for the fact

That she had to exist at all

Her only wish was to protect us

From you till I was able

To do so on my own

That time has come

In this moment I am Lilith

And I reject your rotten fruit

I spit it out in disgust for I had

Gorged myself on in it just yesterday

When your illusions still fooled me

But not today now I know

The truth and I am mortified

All I have left to say is thank you

For showing me your true face

Now I can walk away

I don't belong here

I may place one foot back

Briefly for balance

But I'll never go back

To where I came from

I'm happy for you

But still grieving for the little girl

Who was trapped with you

And didn't learn what she needed

To keep herself safe

-HOLDING SPACE-

When you feel

The weight of change

Return to the breath

Let it guide you

As you grieve

What could have been

"INNER EXPLORATION"

Don't be afraid

To play

With the lions

The hard part isn't

Living in the moment

The hard part is

Making the choice to

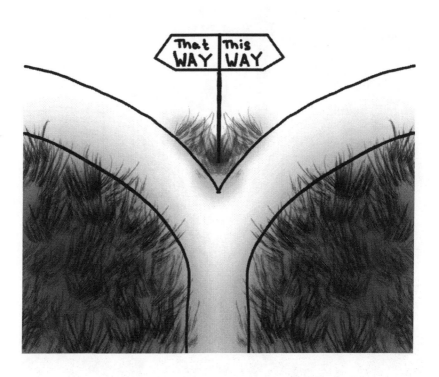

If I was outside

The human experience

Free floating outside

Space and time

Why would I fear

Floating away

Why do I yearn

To float and fear it

All at the same time

Maybe trauma causes

Us to cling to the ground

Maybe a balance

Of both is necessary

To fully experience

Being human

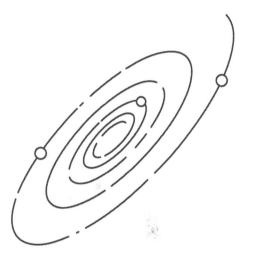

"Don't worry, Sister
I know where to go."

-ELDER SISTER

I stand face to face

With Mother Nature

Knowing that if

I turn away

All will be lost

And away I'll wither

To nothingness

The calibration

Is happening

At a higher level

Your spiritual beliefs

Are yours Love

And they should always

Be uniquely yours

I just want to sit

Here together

And map out Our stars

I'm sorry

I've been short

I've had all

Of humanity

On my mind

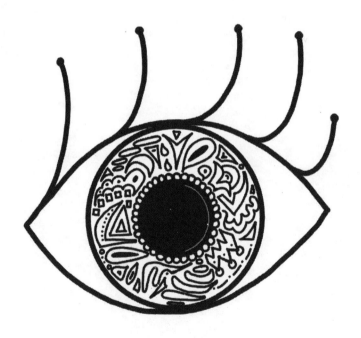

I'm learning how to surrender

To the understanding that

I'll often have no idea

Where it is I'm going

I'll have my time

To live in the cosmos

And meet my creator

But for now I'll live

For this very moment

The land you till

Will never produce

What you haven't earned

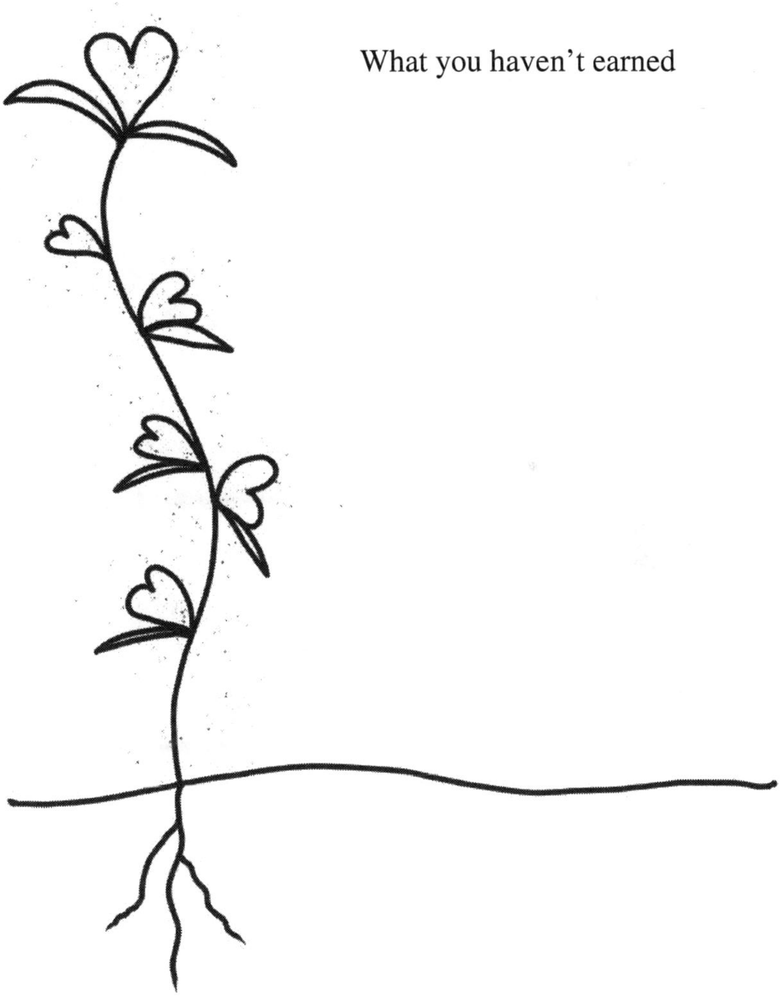

Healing happens

In the space

You hold for yourself

It amuses me

To talk about

What is

Because

What is

Is all there is

To talk about

Practice in the light

And you'll succeed

In the dark

Earth is my classroom

And life is my teacher

Gratitude gifts us

The opportunity

To hold space

For duality

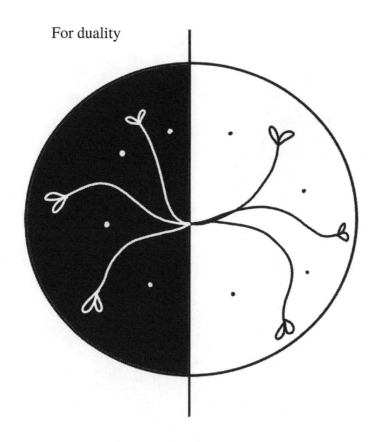

I am the daughter

Of Mother Earth

I am the Heathen Priestess

-WAR CRY-

Today I awoke

With the smell of

Salts and sage

Still lingering on my skin

-BLISS-

Sister,

My promise is to

Hold space for you

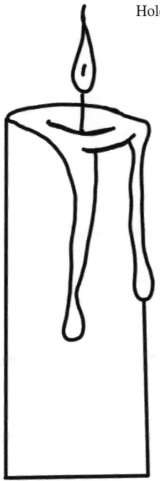

Instead of asking our children

What they want to be

Let's ask them

Who they want to be

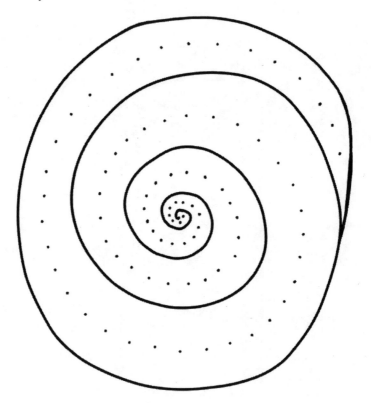

We are raising

Creators of the universe

Act like it

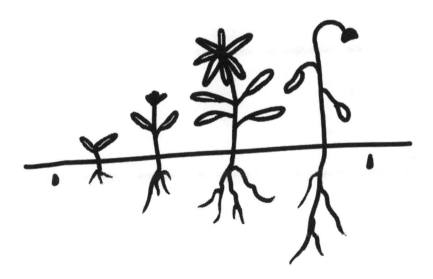

Every child

Deserves a parent

Who strives not

To get stuck

In the Illusion

Generations from now

My granddaughters and grandsons

Will carry with them a part of me

That I tore the universe open to find

"MANTRA &SELF"

BE OPEN

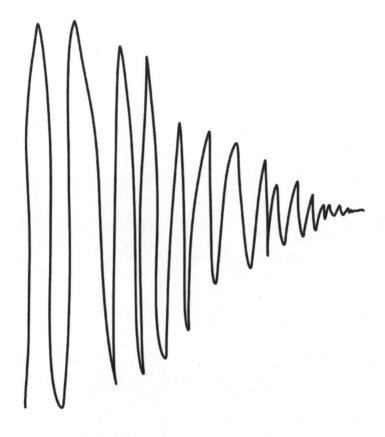

SLOW DOWN

What happens

When your God

Grows bored

With You?

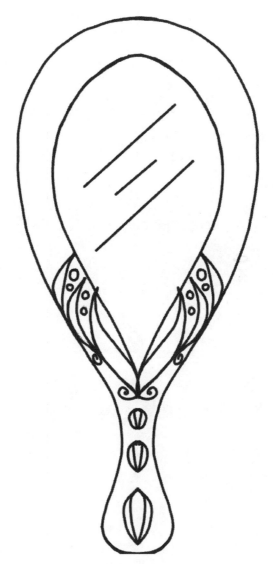

WHAT IS THE TRUTH OF ME?

Let your heart

Crack wide open

You are here

To have the human experience

Not be it

I Bleed Red

Just Like You

I DON'T WANT

A PRE-LIVED LIFE

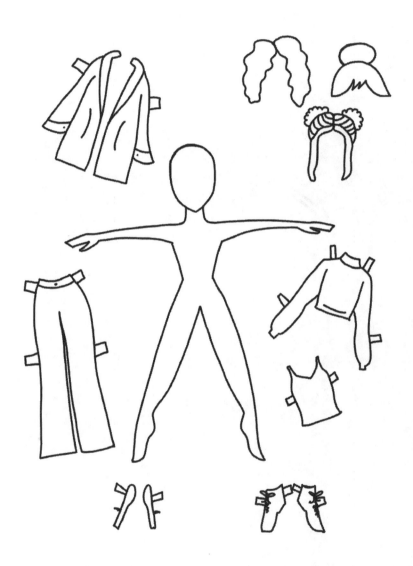

Everything

Is sacred when

Nothing

Is taken for granted

REST

Some battles

Are too big

To fight

All at once

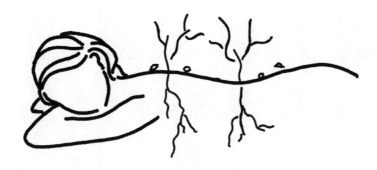

ALLOW YOURSELF TO RECEIVE

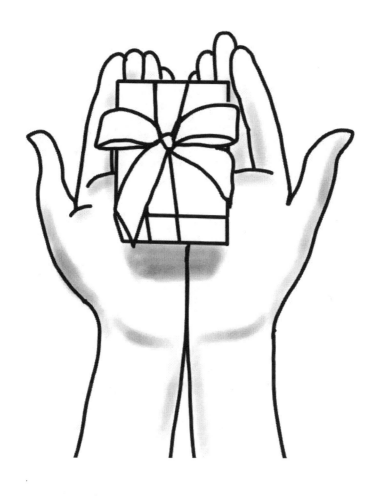

It's your journey
ENJOY

IF ONLY MORE PEOPLE
WERE TAUGHT HOW TO LOVE

WAIT

For the moment of truth

It's not how guarded

I have to be

It's how vulnerable

I'm willing to be

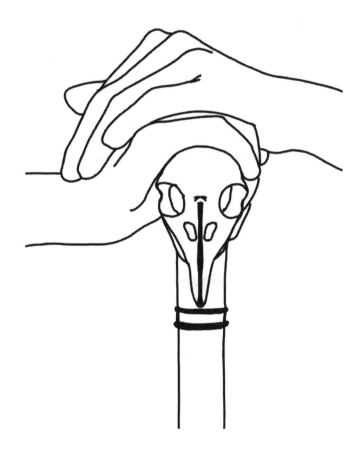

"YOU ARE THE MAGIC"

-SOURCE

Quit feeding it

And it will die

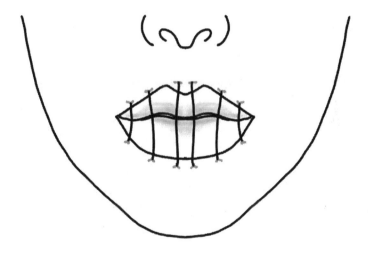

"Don't let anyone rush you"
-Father
(the only advice I kept)

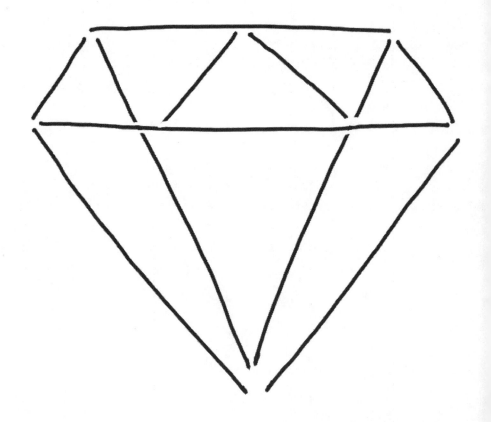

DARKNESS
HUMBLES US

LESS STRESS MORE FUN

The breath

Is my sacred contract

With life

You have

All the time

You need

IF YOU SEEK

YOU ARE WORTHY

I am I am I am I am
I am I am I am I am
I am I am I am I am
Am /am,əm/
first person singular present of _BE_
Be /bē/
exist. occur; take place
I am I am I am I am
I am I am I am I am
I am I am I am I am

"LOVERS"

"Call me Daddy
And we will solve
Those sex issues"

-Lover

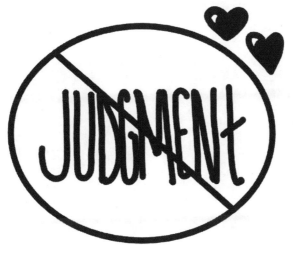

I love you
Take my body
No its not my heart
But im trying

It's in pieces
On the floor here
Take a step back
No don't go there

Jagged
And sharp
Don't know what's next
That's just my heart

Wait don't move
Oh God
I've cut you
That will leave a scar

You should run now
Don't look back
It's gone now
What we had

I've lit the match
All will be ash soon
It all must die
But not you

What goes up
Must come down

Here we go again
Round and round

Faster Slower
You know my body

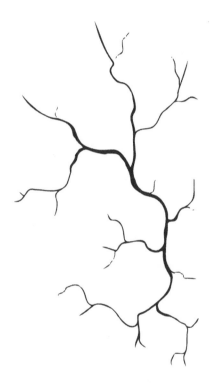

It speaks to you
Without trying

Follow me here
You know you will

It's not good for you
Only I can tell

Try to stop now
But I want more

Legs open
Take me on the floor

Nothing but sweat
Is between us

Hold me this way
And you know what's next

My nails drag
Down your back

Fuck I'm sorry
I've done it again

On a Thursday the grass grows
And the wind blows

On a Thursday your blue eyes
Show me all I need to know

On a Thursday the world looks new
With nothing to do

Slow down, take it in
This day will never come again
Drink the juice while it's sweet
Kiss the ground under your feet

On a Thursday winds will change
There is nothing left to gain

On a Thursday night will fall
And you'll have to answer the call

On a Thursday she will leave and
It won't be what it seems

Slow down, take it in
This day will never come again
Drink the juice while it's sweet
Kiss the ground under your feet

On a Thursday the sun will rise
Come now dry your eyes

On a Thursday flowers bloom and
The bees will find them soon

On a Thursday you'll catch your breath
It only feels like death

Slow down, take it in
This day will never come again
Drink the juice while it's sweet
Kiss the ground under your feet

Own me
But don't stifle me

Possess me
But don't cage me

Love me
But don't guilt me

Buzz Buzz goes the bee
If only we could see what he sees

Every story has two sides
What would it look like through his eyes

Hover soft hover slow
Never knowing how the wind will blow

Easy does it gentle touch
You will kill it if you clutch

The rain threatens flight
Close your eyes and hold on tight

Wait, that's what got us here
Will the answer ever be clear

The flowers perfume so toxic
Longing so much to touch it

But the garden wasn't ours
The sign read "permanent scar"

Buzz buzz goes the bee
Staring straight at you and me

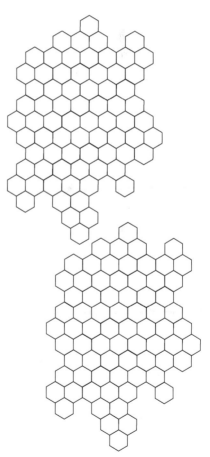

I'll scrub down the walls

I'll mop up the blood

I'll bury the bodies

Won't look up till it's done

I'm growing

I'm learning

I'm sorry

Can't be US

Till I clean up this mess

Stop offering sex

To help him feel better

Your eyes meet mine
They take it all
My breath My tone My hurt My sigh

Your eyes meet mine
They tell it all
Your heat Your drive Your heart Your soul

Your eyes meet mine
They feel it all
Our touch Our light Our link Our love

The wind keeps blowing through
You're staring at me unsure what to do

I close my eyes and welcome the winds arrival
When I open them I witness you unravel

Like the flip of a switch and I don't understand
This is what I've waited for it's part of the plan

Breathe it's ok I've got you
I will never leave you

Follow my steps this way I'll lead
Just as you've done for me when I'm in need

Throw yourself into the gusts
Lets see where it takes us

If you need to put your feet down
To find solid ground for a moment or two

That's ok
I'll put my feet down too

Like a flash in the night
We collide

Like a smokey sky
We lose our sight

Like a shooting star
We burn hot then fizzle

Like a match just struck
We rekindle

Like a baby's first smile
We see we can be new

Like the sun and the moon
We know all it takes is me and you

Your lips are sweet as sin
I'll kiss them now and then again

Strip down so I can see
All it is you hide from me

Salty Sweat under my tongue
Your skin always makes me come undone

Words slip between your lips
They soothe my soul mmm just like this

Your fingers trace my face
Yes please my favorite place

Body to body now
I breathe you in and wonder how

Someone could feel like home
I'm right here you're not alone

Hands in your hair lips everywhere
Your eyes catch mine and I just stare

I love us just like this
Tangled together in perfect bliss

Thank You

**UNRAVELING
WITH RAYNE**

2022